DEDICATION

My goal is to enrich the lives of children everywhere by helping them to discover valuable lessons through stories, music, and art. I dedicate this book to parents, friends, family members and educators everywhere who share this vision in our collective effort to make the world a better place for generations to come.

This book is also dedicated to my own late Mother and Father who always encouraged me to be myself. I'm still in awe at how dedicated they were to successfully raising seven children. Among other qualities, my mother with her unconditional love and acceptance taught me to love, and my father with his endless sense of humor taught me to laugh. Thank you for providing me with the foundation to learn my own lessons in life - I will forever be influenced by your wisdom, love, and support.

Bobby Priest

MUSICAL READ-ALONG SERIES

AGES 3-8

I can READ

I can SING

MUSICAL READ-ALONG SERIES

This book is even more magical when it's read along with the music of the accompanying lullaby. Additionally, children of all ages will enjoy the Bop Bop Bunny Dance Song

Visit our YouTube Channel to listen to: "The Planets Lullaby" The "Bop Bop" Song

Visit www.litlbobby.com

CHORUS

"Lit'l Bobby learns lessons
and wonderful things
from The Voice of The Moon
every night as she sings"
[Repeat]

Where this icon appears
STOP and sing the chorus

SING CHORUS

A Musical Bedtime Story for the Young at Heart

Conceived and Written by Bobby Priest
Music and Lyrics by Bobby Priest
Illustrations by Anna Methers
Volume Two of Seven / ISBN-978-1-7342714-2-3

THE VOICE OF THE MOON
THE PLANETS

By Bobby Priest

Lit'l Bobby asleep the Moon started to rise
Bop Bop Bunny watched as she lit up the skies.

Do you know about planets like Venus and Mars?
They're all friends of mine and so are the stars.

Some planets are big and some planets are small they float in the sky but somehow they don't fall.

They hide in the day but we see them at night because during the day they get lost in the light.

Most we can't see them with only our eyes
with telescope lenses we peek in the skies.

With a magical scope it all becomes real
So let's look very closely and see what we will.

SING
CHORUS

Please tell me more Bobby said with surprise
I want to meet all your friends in the skies.

What are they like please I really must know
are there oceans and mountains and do they have snow?

Let's meet all my friends and let's name every one
let's start with a star that we call the Sun.

The planets they circle the Sun in the sky
like spokes on a wheel round and round they do fly.

Right next to the Sun, Mercury is his name
he's the smallest of planets with craters and plains.

He's the fastest of all and shines golden red light and he's scorching by day but he freezes at night.

SING CHORUS

Venus is next she's the hottest we know
with big lava rocks her volcanos they flow.

She used to have water it all boiled away
and now she's as dry as the desert at day.

The vast Mother Earth she's my favorite of all
she's covered with oceans her land is quite small.

She supports life where the others have none
I light up her night and by day she has sun.

Mars the red planet sometimes we can see
with one giant mountain as tall as can be.

He also has canyons and craters and plains
his dust storms they cover his surface like rain.

SING
CHORUS

Jupiter's next he's a giant you know
his storms they are fierce as they blow to and fro.

With a swirling red spot that he makes with his winds
he has 64 moons and they all are my friends.

Saturn has colorful rings all around
they come from his rainbows of ice on the ground.

They twirl great colors so beautifully
with at least 18 moons the last planet we see.

Uranus is dim in the distance he hides
the coldest of planets he's frozen inside.

He has many moons of which Cupid is one
his color is blue and he's seventh from the Sun.

SING
CHORUS

Neptune is last of the planets we know
named after the sea with a brilliant blue glow.

He has 14 moons of which Triton is one
the furthest of planets he's eighth from the Sun.

Of the planets we know you may think there are nine
Pluto was one in a previous time.
He didn't fit in so he doesn't exist
now there's no longer 9 there's just 8 on the list.

No one's the same we're all different you know
but that's perfectly fine said the Moon with a glow.
Maybe someday all the planets will say
he's still one of us and we want him to stay.

SING
CHORUS

Most stars live in galaxies ever so far
where the Milky Way flows like a river of stars.

They all gather 'round so far and so high
you can see them at night as they light up the sky.

Now that you know all the planets there are
and the center of all is the sunniest star.

Let us learn all their names like the friends we do keep
as you lay on your pillow and drift off to sleep.

Venus

Earth

Sun

Mercury

The Sun is a star and Mercury's fast,
Venus is hot, Mother Earth she is vast.
Mars he is red, Jupiter has a spot
Saturn has rings made of rainbows he's got.

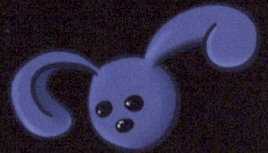

SING
CHORUS

Mars

Jupiter

Uranus

Neptune

Saturn

Uranus is cold with ice to his core
Neptune is last with a brilliant blue glow.
They live in this great, "Solar System" we say
where they shine in the night and they hide in the day.

Now that you've met all my friends in the skies
think of their names as you close both your eyes.

Breathe ever so softly don't utter a peep
as you lay on your pillow and drift off to sleep.

The Moon asked Lit'l Bobby, "if you lived in the sky which one would you be and please tell me why?"

THE END

Lit'l Bobby replied as he gazed from his room
"I'd be Mother Earth to be close to the Moon."

SING
CHORUS

About the author

A California Native, and youngest of seven children, Bobby Priest (A.K.A. Robert William Priest) graduated with honors from the University of California San Diego. During his time at UCSD, his honors thesis centered around a remedial reading program for children. He went on to earn an MBA from California Polytechnic State University, San Luis Obispo, where he served as President of the MBA Association. His professional experience that followed was focused primarily in Finance, International Real Estate, and authoring a popular weekly Financial Newspaper Column.

In a serious leap of faith, inspired by his lifelong love for music and the loss and memories of his beloved parents, Bobby left his life in Corporate America. He set out upon a journey dedicated to following his passion for writing books and music. This path eventually led him to the most creative place in the world that he could imagine - Bali, Indonesia.

Bobby is now focused on combining his love for writing books and music with the children's book series, 'The Voice of the Moon.' This unique educational series for children combines important life lessons with music in a fun and entertaining way. Although Bobby loves to entertain kids with his books and songs, as a singer and songwriter, he also continues to write and perform his unique style of original acoustic mainstream music.

BobbyPriest.com

www.ingramcontent.com/pod-product-compliance
Lightning Source LLC
Chambersburg PA
CBHW041547040426
42447CB00002B/73